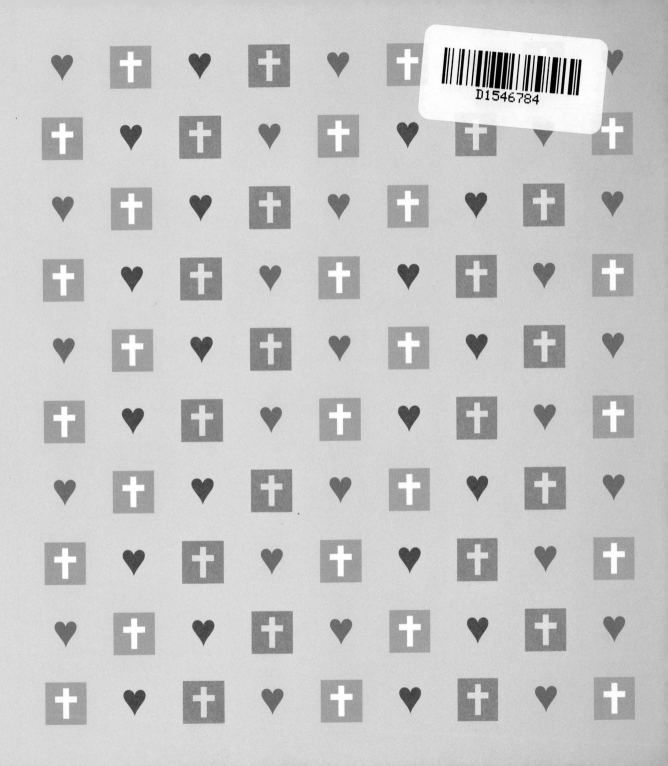

An Ark Full of ANIMALS

Written by
RENITA BOYLE

Illustrated by
HONOR AYRES

ASCENSION
Kids

West Chester, PA

First edition 2013 under the title
Not a Cloud in the Sky.

This edition published 2021 by Ascension Publishing Group, LLC.

Copyright © 2013 Anno Domini Publishing.
www.ad-publishing.com

Text copyright © 2013 Renita Boyle.
Illustrations copyright © 2013 Honor Ayres.

Editorial review for Ascension by Amy Welborn.

Ascension
PO Box 1990
West Chester, PA 19380
www.ascensionpress.com
1-800-376-0520
ISBN 978-1-950784-78-3
Printed in the United States of America
21 22 23 24 25 5 4 3 2 1

"But I will establish my covenant with you; and you shall come into the ark, you, your sons, your wife, and your sons' wives with you."

GENESIS 6:18

1

There was not a cloud in the sky.
There was no sign of rain – no drip, no drop,
no plip, no plop, no wind across the plain.
But Noah would build an ark anyway because
he knew what God had planned.

No one believed what God said anymore.
Everyone forgot — everyone but Noah;
Noah did not!

"I made a wonderful world," God said, "and people to get along. Now they do all kinds of evil things, and everything's gone wrong. Although it makes me very sad, I'm going to start again. There's

going to be a great big flood and I need your help, old friend. We're going to build a great big ark. I'll tell you what to do. Your family will be safe on board, and lots of animals too!"

6

So Noah and Mrs. Noah, their three sons and their wives — they all began to build the Ark that would one day save their lives.

Bang, bang! went the hammer.

Zip, zip! went the saw.

Up, up went the great big Ark, so tall and long and wide, with a roof, a door and windows, and lots of rooms inside.

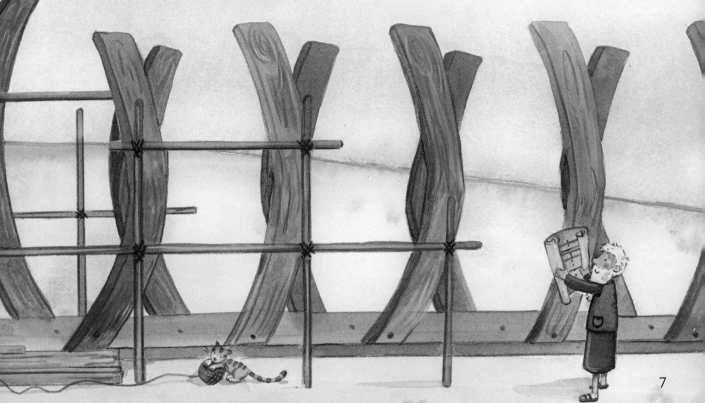

It took years and years to build that Ark.
People laughed at Noah and stared.

"We will trust the Lord and get on board,"
said Noah. But no one really cared.

"You're crazy!" they all said.
"What you say is a lie!
How can there be a flood when
there is not a cloud in the sky?!"

Then one day, when the work was done,
a cloud appeared and covered the sun.

Animals came from all around:
short and tall, thin and round.
Some were smooth and some were hairy;
some were sweet and some were scary!

Crawling, hopping, flipping, flopping, they marched and scampered and flew. Two by two by two by two, they marched and scampered and flew up the ramp and through the door, across the squeaky, creaky floor into the many rooms inside the great big Ark, so tall and long and wide. Noah's family settled in too.

The more the clouds gathered, the darker it grew, until it was dark as darkest night. **Ba boom!** went the thunder. The door **banged** tight.

Plip, plop on the pointy roof; drip, drop against the door. Flish, flash, splish, splash — it pittered, it pattered, it poured!

For forty days and forty nights, rain thrashed down from the sky — but all inside the bobbing Ark stayed warm and safe and dry.

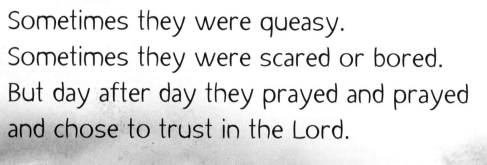

Sometimes they were queasy.
Sometimes they were scared or bored.
But day after day they prayed and prayed
and chose to trust in the Lord.

They took care of each other and the animals too.
They did the work that God gave them to do.

Then one day, the rain just stopped.
God sent a breeze to blow, and slowly,
slowly, very slowly, the water began to go.
But months and months and months went
past before the world was dry at last.

And though the wait was very long, Noah's faith was very strong because he knew what God had planned.

Old Noah laughed and skipped and juMPed when at last they bumped onto a great, tall mountain!

Up went the window, in came the sun, out went a dove to find dry ground. The dove came back with a branch from a tree. **"Hooray!"** said all Noah's family.

And when God said, "Come on out!"
all of the animals gave a shout – roaring,
crowing, squeaking, chirping, buzzing, howling,
grunting, purring.
Crawling, hopping, flipping, flopping,
they marched and scampered and flew.

Two by two by two by two, they marched
and scampered and flew across the floor and
out of the door into the world so new.

Then Noah, Mrs. Noah,
their three sons and their
wives stopped to thank
their amazing God for saving
all their lives.

Then in the sky above them
a rainbow began to shine.

"I'll never flood the whole earth again,"
God promised. "Every rainbow will be a sign."

In that Ark, God had saved them from the flood. He'd rescued them from all the sadness and sin. Now it was time for a brand new life to begin!

Noah looked up beyond the rainbow:
there was not a cloud in the sky.

"When the bow is in the clouds, I will look upon it and remember the everlasting covenant between God and every living creature of all flesh that is upon the earth."

GENESIS 9:16

AND THAT IS *The End* OF THIS
STORY ... BUT NOT THE END OF *Your Story*.
Peace be with you!